Make it easy...
English
Age 8-9

Alison Head

Two-syllable words

Thinking about how we say a word can help us to spell it.

If a word with two syllables has a long vowel sound in the middle, the vowel is followed by a single consonant.

ho**p**ing

If it has a short vowel sound in the middle, the vowel is followed by a double consonant.

ho**pp**ing

The only exception to this rule is words starting *mod*, which never have a double consonant.

model

I Say each word out loud to help you decide the type of vowel sound it has. Then tick the correct box.

	long vowel sound	short vowel sound			long vowel sound	short vowel sound
a pile	☐	☐		f puppy	☐	☐
b bitter	☐	☐		g taping	☐	☐
c happy	☐	☐		h writing	☐	☐
d sorry	☐	☐		i holly	☐	☐
e super	☐	☐		j liner	☐	☐

II Write these sentences again, spelling the words correctly.

a There are aple and chery trees in my garden.

_____

b I grabed the kiten. _____

c My house is more moddern than your cotage.

_____

d John scribled on the papper. _____

e Mum read what was writen on the labbel.

_____

f The rabit was runing all over the garden.

_____

Homophones

Homophones are words that sound the same, but have different meanings or spellings.

You need to think about the whole sentence to know which is the right word to use.

flour   flower

We bought some **flour** to bake the cake.

I picked a red **flower**.

I Write homophones for these words.

a knew _____
b hole _____
c grate _____
d there _____
e two _____

f herd _____
g sea _____
h be _____
i for _____
j write _____

II Write a sentence for each homophone to show you know how to use it correctly.

a plaice _We had plaice and chips._
b place _I know the place you mean._
c threw _____
d through _____
e son _____
f sun _____
g floor _____
h flaw _____
i main _____
j mane _____

Regular verb endings

Verbs tell us what a person or thing is doing. The ending of the **verb** changes depending on who is doing the activity and whether it has already happened (past), is happening now (present) or will happen (future).

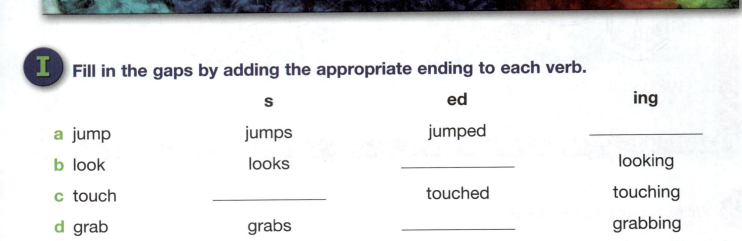

    she walked   she walks   she will be walking

Sometimes the spelling of the verb changes when the ending is added.

I Fill in the gaps by adding the appropriate ending to each verb.

	s	ed	ing
a jump	jumps	jumped	_____
b look	looks	_____	looking
c touch	_____	touched	touching
d grab	grabs	_____	grabbing
e shop	shops	shopped	_____
f save	saves	_____	_____
g cry	_____	cried	_____

II Write these sentences again, using the correct form of the verb in bold.

a The car **stops** a few seconds ago at the traffic lights.
_____

b Dad was **cooked** the chips when we got home.
_____

c I **carrying** the shopping home for Gran yesterday.
_____

d Mum always **washing** the car on Saturdays after we go swimming.
_____

e Freddie **drops** the rubbish in the bin before he left the park.
_____

f Jenny always **exploring** the rock pools as soon as she gets to the beach.
_____

Suffixes

We can add suffixes to the **ends** of some words to change their meaning.

ship, *ness* and *ment* are all suffixes we can add without changing the spelling of the root word.

> sponsor + **ship** = sponsorship
>
> fair + **ness** = fairness
>
> battle + **ment** = battlement

The only exception is if the word ends in a consonant followed by *y*, when you change the *y* to *i* before adding the suffix.

> tidy + **ness** = tidiness

I Complete these word sums.

a partner + ship = _____

b kind + ness = _____

c fit + ness = _____

d enjoy + ment = _____

e willing + ness = _____

f member + ship = _____

g silly + ness = _____

h friend + ship = _____

i careless + ness = _____

j amuse + ment = _____

II Choose *ship*, *ness* or *ment* to add to each of these words. Then write down the new word.

a measure _____

b tidy _____

c nasty _____

d employ _____

e state _____

f wicked _____

g fellow _____

h apprentice _____

i replace _____

j champion _____

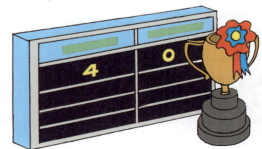

5

Definitions

A definition is a **description** of what a word means.

cat: a four-legged furry animal, often kept as a pet.

I Draw a line to match up these words with their definitions.

a house — a piece of land used for farming
b sheep — a fruit grown on trees
c bed — a farmyard animal producing milk
d breakfast — a building people live in
e field — the coldest season
f apple — a farmyard animal producing wool
g winter — the first meal of the day
h cow — a piece of furniture used for sleeping on

II Write your own definition for each word.

 a shoe _____

 b camera _____

 c vase _____

 d kettle _____

 e clock _____

 f school _____

Alphabetical order

Putting words in alphabetical order helps us to find information in dictionaries and indexes.

If the first two letters of a group of words are the same, we can use the third and fourth letters to put the words in alphabetical order.

baby   baggage   ball

a **b** c d e f **g** h i j k **l** m n o p q r s t u v w x y z

I Use the third bold letter to find the whole word in the box. Then write in the missing letters so the words are in alphabetical order. The first one has been done for you.

sunny   super   suspect   submarine   sudden
summer   sugar   suitable   success

a sub**m**arine
b suc_____
c sud_____

d sug_____
e sui_____
f sum_____

g sun_____
h sup_____
i sus_____

II Write these words again in alphabetical order, using the third and fourth letters.

hair   hare   hat   hail
harp   hard   haste   have

a _____
b _____
c _____
d _____

e _____
f _____
g _____
h _____

Rhyming words

Rhyming words have the same sound at the end.

shop   mop   top

I Sort these words into their correct rhyming groups.

chair   tight   moat   boat   pair   height   stair   bite   stoat
rare   goat   bear   kite   float   bright

Words that rhyme with **light**   Words that rhyme with **coat**   Words that rhyme with **hair**

a _____   b _____   c _____

_____   _____   _____

_____   _____   _____

_____   _____   _____

II Look at each word. Now write down another three that rhyme with it.

a look   _____   _____   _____

b sweet   _____   _____   _____

c trot   _____   _____   _____

d rear   _____   _____   _____

e bread   _____   _____   _____

f beach   _____   _____   _____

Making verbs

We can turn some nouns and adjectives into verbs by adding suffixes like *ate*, *en*, *ify* or *ise*.

With most words you can just add the suffix. If the word already has a suffix, or ends in *e* or *y*, the suffix or final letter must usually be removed before you add the new suffix.

deaf + **en** = deafen

quantity − **ity** = quant
quant + **ify** = quantify

I Complete these word sums to make new verbs.

a deep + en = _____

b short + en = _____

c standard + ise = _____

d apology + ise = _____

e note + ify = _____

f elastic + ate = _____

g pure + ify = _____

h formal + ise = _____

i wake + en = _____

j medic + ate = _____

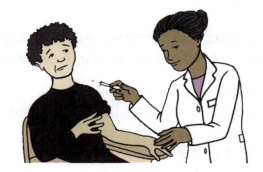

II Add *ate*, *en*, *ify* or *ise* to these words to make verbs. Then write the words out in full.

a intense + _____ = _____

b real + _____ = _____

c strength + _____ = _____

d simple + _____ = _____

e hard + _____ = _____

f glory + _____ = _____

g haste + _____ = _____

h class + _____ = _____

i serial + _____ = _____

j weak + _____ = _____

Irregular verbs

When verbs are used to tell us what a person or thing has already done, most end in *ed*. This is called the past tense.

Present
I **look** at the book.

Past
Yesterday I **looked** at the book.

Some verbs have their own spelling patterns, especially in the past tense. These are known as irregular verbs.

I **keep** rabbits.   I **kept** rabbits.

I The past tense verbs in these sentences are wrongly spelt. Write the verb correctly.

a I hurted my hand.

b Sam putted his toys away.

c Claire runned home.

d Mum bringed my tea.

e I sended you a letter.

f The autumn leaves falled from the trees.

II Write these sentences again. Start with the words in bold type and make sure the past tense verb is spelt correctly. The first one has been done for you.

a I eat my birthday cake.
Yesterday, I ate my birthday cake.

b Jamilla buys a comic.
Last week,

c Ali draws a picture.
Earlier today,

d I am tired.
Last night,

e I can swim.
When I was four,

f I tell you a secret.
Yesterday,

Adverbs

Adverbs tell us how a person or thing does something.

I walked **quickly** to school.

The fish swam **energetically**.

I Underline the adverbs in these sentences.

a Ashley carefully dusted the china.
b The choir sang beautifully.
c The snow fell silently all around us.
d Bees buzzed lazily round the flowers.
e The cake was badly burnt.
f Asif ate his lunch happily.
g Craig yawned sleepily.
h Imogen shouted angrily at her brother.
i We waited impatiently.

II Think of a suitable adverb to complete these sentences.

a The mouse scurried _____ away.
b My sister stormed _____ from the room.
c Gemma thought _____ about the maths problem.
d The star shone _____ in the sky.
e Liam dawdled _____ home.
f Jess _____ scribbled down the phone number.
g My naughty brother behaved _____.
h Dad patted the dog _____.
i We talked _____ in the library.

Powerful verbs

Verbs tell us what a person or thing is doing.

The dog runs.

Powerful verbs also tell us **how** a person or thing does something. Sometimes they tell us so much, we do not need adverbs.

The dog runs quickly.

The dog sprints.

I Sort each verb into its correct group. Then add two more of your own to each group.

hobbles argues devours munches shuffles dictates chews declares ambles

walks **says** **eats**

a _____ b _____ c _____

II Read the fairytale. Then choose a powerful verb from the box to use instead of the verbs and adverbs in brackets.

Jack and his mother were very poor. One day, Jack's mother (sternly told) _____ him to sell their cow. When he sold it for a handful of beans, Jack's mother (shouted loudly) _____ at him.

Overnight, a magic beanstalk (grew rapidly) _____ up into the clouds. Jack (climbed quickly) _____ to the top and (walked quietly) _____ past the sleeping giant.

As Jack (looked longingly) _____ at some bags of gold, the giant woke up, so he (quickly collected) _____ the gold and (ran away) _____ down the beanstalk.

When he reached the bottom, Jack's mother (cut quickly) _____ away at the beanstalk. The giant (fell heavily) _____ to the ground, and Jack and his mother lived happily ever after.

grabbed
shot
ordered
crashed
yelled
clambered
fled
hacked
gazed
crept

Commas

Commas show us when to **pause** in a sentence.

They are also useful for **breaking up** longer sentences.

Which is your coat, Alex?

Jo, my friend, is eight years old.

 Add the missing commas to these sentences.

a After tea we played football.
b Find your trainers Paul.
c Suddenly the lights went out.
d Judy and James from next door came shopping with us.
e My hat which is black matches my scarf.
f Last Tuesday after school I went skating.

 Write these sentences again, putting the commas in the correct place.

a Tomorrow we, are playing football.
_____

b The ink which, was blue stained, the carpet.
_____

c Eventually Jane, won the game.
_____

d It's, time to go Ali.
_____

e While we were on, holiday we stayed in a hotel.
_____

f At, school in my classroom is a display about, trains.
_____

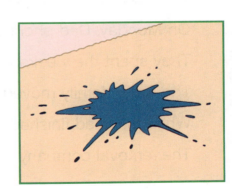

Chronology

When we write something, it is important for the reader to be able to tell the order in which things happen.

I   **Number these pictures 1 to 6 to put the cartoon strip in the right order.**

II   **Write these sentences again in the right order to make a short story. Then add your own sentence about what you think happened next.**

On Monday, Dad phoned the removal company to see if they had the box.

They spent the weekend unpacking.

The Smith family moved into their new house on Friday.

When they had finished unpacking, Grace realised that a box of her toys was missing.

The removal company looked in the van and found the box.

a _____

b _____

c _____

d _____

e _____

f _____

Tricky plurals

Plural means **more than one** of something.

When you spell plurals, there are rules you have to follow.

Words ending in *f* usually change to *ves* in the plural.

Words ending *ff* just add *s*.

leaf

lea**ves**

cu**ff**

cu**ff**s

I Underline the correct plural spelling for each word.

a **sniff**   snives   snifs   sniffs
b **half**   halves   halfs   halffs
c **puff**   puves   pufs   puffs
d **cliff**   clifs   clives   cliffs
e **scarf**   scarves   scarfs   scuves
f **scuff**   scufs   scuffs   scuves
g **calf**   calves   calfs   calffs
h **thief**   thiefs   thieves   thiefes
i **yourself** yourselfs yourselves yourselff
j **knife**   knifes   kniffes   knives

II Write down the plural form of these words.

a loaf   _____   f wife   _____

b self   _____   g bluff   _____

c sheriff _____   h shelf   _____

d cuff   _____   i elf   _____

e wolf   _____   j scoff   _____

Choosing words

Choosing the right words for your writing is important.

Some words don't tell us very much.

> We had a **good** time at the party.

Other words are more powerful and tell us much more.

> We had a **fantastic** time at the party.

I Draw lines to match these words with a more interesting alternative.

a hungry   hilarious
b tired   terrifying
c nice   parched
d nasty   horrible
e scary   starving
f dry   lovely
g wet   exhausted
h funny   drenched

II Write these sentences again, choosing a better word to replace the words in bold.

a It is **hot** today.

_____

b We **got** some crisps at the shop.

_____

c Kate **made** some biscuits.

_____

d The mouse was **small**.

_____

e We had lunch and **then** we went to the cinema.

_____

Changing language

The words we use change over time.

gramophone: an old-fashioned piece of equipment.

satellite: a modern piece of equipment.

I Sort these words and phrases into older and newer groups. Use a dictionary to help you.

	older	newer			older	newer
a frock	☐	☐	f yonder	☐	☐
b compact disc	☐	☐	g fast food	☐	☐
c shilling	☐	☐	h behold	☐	☐
d mangle	☐	☐	i website	☐	☐
e Internet	☐	☐	j online	☐	☐

II Write down a more modern way of saying these things.

a We drove in the automobile.

_____

b From whence did you come?

_____

c Behold the wondrous sight.

_____

d Wilt thou tarry awhile?

_____

e Shall we listen to the wireless?

_____

f It was cold so I wore a muffler.

_____

Making adjectives

Adjectives **describe** things or people. We can often make adjectives by adding a suffix to a noun or verb.

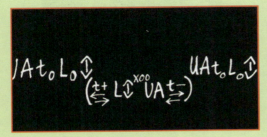

bore + ing = bor**ing**

beauty + ful = beaut**iful**

Words ending in a single *e* drop the *e* when adding *ing* or *able*.

Words ending in *y* change the *y* to *i* when adding *ful* or *able*.

I Complete these word sums to turn these nouns and verbs into adjectives.

a shock + ing = _____

b wash + able = _____

c trust + worthy = _____

d beauty + ful = _____

e rely + able = _____

f acid + ic = _____

g road + worthy = _____

h amuse + ing = _____

i break + able = _____

j pain + ful = _____

II Choose *ful* or *able* to complete these word sums. Then write the words out in full.

a wish + _____ = _____

b agree + _____ = _____

c envy + _____ = _____

d hope + _____ = _____

e wonder + _____ = _____

f care + _____ = _____

g adore + _____ = _____

h help + _____ = _____

i value + _____ = _____

j mercy + _____ = _____

More adjectives

Adjectives can help us to compare things or people.

Comparative adjectives compare two things – bigger, smaller.

Kate's cat is **bigger** than mine.

Superlative adjectives describe the limit of a quality – biggest, smallest, most enormous.

But Mina's cat is the **biggest** of all.

I Decide whether the adjective in each sentence is comparative or superlative. Then tick the right box.

		comparative	superlative
a	This winter is the coldest on record.	☐	☐
b	I live closer to the school than you do.	☐	☐
c	I chose the least difficult question.	☐	☐
d	My sister is younger than me.	☐	☐
e	We saw the longest snake at the zoo.	☐	☐
f	Diamonds are more valuable than pearls.	☐	☐
g	My house is bigger than yours.	☐	☐
h	The theme park was the most exciting place I've ever been.	☐	☐

II Complete the chart by adding the missing comparative and superlative adjectives.

	comparative adjectives	superlative adjectives
a	taller	_____
b	_____	narrowest
c	more amazing	_____
d	_____	best
e	older	_____
f	_____	most delicious
g	stranger	_____
h	_____	least interesting

Apostrophes for contraction

If two words are used together a lot, we can sometimes join them together. We do this by taking out some of the letters and putting an apostrophe in their place.

do not → don't

I am → I'm

I Cross out the incorrect shortened form from the words in bold.

a **It's Its'** my birthday tomorrow.

b Jake is off school today because **hes he's** ill.

c I **didn't did'nt** do my homework.

d Unless we hurry **wel'l we'll** miss the bus.

e Dad **wo'nt won't** be home until later.

f My brother **wouldn't would'nt** let me watch TV.

g **You're Your're** my best friend.

h **Theyve They've** forgotten their bags.

II Write these sentences again, replacing the bold words with the correct shortened form.

a We **must not** speak in class.

_____

b You can play football after **you have** done your homework.

_____

c He **should not** have eaten so much cake.

_____

d I **cannot** ice skate very well.

_____

e They **could not** find our house.

_____

More apostrophes

Apostrophes are also used to tell us when something belongs to somebody or something.

With single or collective nouns, the apostrophe usually goes before the s.

With plurals ending in s, the apostrophe usually goes after the s.

The people's shoes   The man's hat

The girls' bags

I Write in the missing apostrophes in these phrases.

a the womans bag
b the boys heads
c the childs toy
d the peoples books
e two dogs baskets
f the suns rays
g two footballers boots
h a cats tail

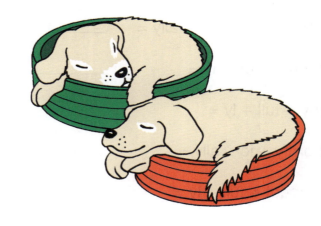

II Write down the shortened form of each phrase.

a the wings of a bird   _____
b the pens belonging to the boys _____
c the cat belonging to Kim   _____
d the parcels belonging to Sam   _____
e the car belonging to my parents _____
f the rattles belonging to the babies _____
g the wallet belonging to my dad _____
h the sweets belonging to the children _____

More suffixes

Sometimes you can add two suffixes to the end of a word.

hope + **ful** + **ly** = hopefully

Sometimes you can add more than one different suffix to a word.

relate + **ion** = relation

relate + **ive** = relative

I Complete these word sums. Remember the spelling rules for adding suffixes.

a grate + full + ly = _____

b converse + ation + ally = _____

c energy + etic + ally = _____

d photograph + ic + ally = _____

e thank + full + ly = _____

f joy + full + ly = _____

g horrify + ic + ally = _____

h respect + full + ly = _____

II Pick two different suffixes from the box that can be added to each of these words. The first one has been done for you.

a correct   correct _ion_____   correct _ly_____

b product   product_____   product_____

c construct construct_____   construct_____

d extreme   extreme_____   extreme_____

e act   act_____   act_____

f real   real_____   real_____

g oppress   oppress_____   oppress_____

h miss   miss_____   miss_____

ive
ly
ion
ist

22

Rhyming patterns

Poets use rhyme in different ways.

Some poems have **alternate rhyming lines.**

Snow falls,
Wind blows,
Bird calls,
Hungry crows.

Some lines rhyme in pairs. These are called **rhyming couplets**.

Sunny days,
Warm rays,
Burning down,
Grass brown.

Some poems use **no rhyme** at all.

Rain splashes,
Wet feet,
Dripping trees,
Black puddles.

 Decide whether each poem has alternate rhyming lines, rhyming couplets or no rhyme.

a

Black night,
Halloween fright,
Bright moon,
A silver balloon.

This poem has

_____

_____

b

Green trees,
Spring leaves,
Fresh-cut grass,
Crunchy apples.

This poem has

_____

_____

c

Red nose,
Warm scarf,
Rosy glows,
Cosy hearth.

This poem has

_____

_____

 Add two lines to each of these poems, making sure you match the rhyming patterns.

a Packed bags,
Luggage tags,
Clutching passport,
Crowded airport,

_____

_____

b Christmas tree,
Gifts below,
Treats for me,
There on show,

_____

_____

Making notes

When we make notes, we only need to write down the **key words**.

I **Underline the key words in each sentence.**

a Molly and Sam are coming to tea.

b I have gone for lunch, but I will be back at noon.

c My birthday is in December.

d Remember you are playing football on Saturday.

e I have Maths and English homework to do.

f We need to buy some milk and bread.

II **Write a full sentence for each set of notes.**

a Tea in oven.

_____

b Brownies, Town Hall, 6pm.

_____

c Lucy's party, Friday, buy gift.

_____

d In garden, come round back.

_____

e Mum rang. Running late.

_____

f Car fixed. Please collect.

_____

Letter strings

Some common letter strings make different sounds in different words.

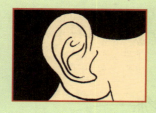
ear

bear

heart

Because they can make different sounds, the words they are found in can be tricky to spell.

I Sort these words into groups containing the same letter string.

aunt   hour   twice   route   sausage   practice
apprentice   shout   autumn   rice   journey   sauce

ou	au	ice
a _____	b _____	c _____

II Match each word with one from the box that has the same letter string and the same sound.

a tough   rough
b trough   _____
c bough   _____
d thought   _____
e bear   _____

f earn   _____
g dear   _____
h freight   _____
i night   _____
j sleight   _____

wear	height
learn	gear
rough	weight
bought	light
plough	cough

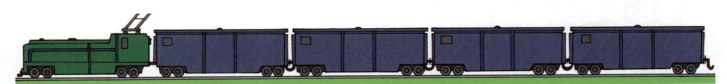

Diminutives

Diminutives are words that describe **small** people, animals or things.

Some diminutives are made by adding a prefix like *mini* or *micro*.

Some are formed by adding a suffix like *let, ette* or *ling*.

minibus

pig**let**

I Add the prefix *mini* or *micro* to these words to form diminutives.

a _____ + film = _____
b _____ + bus = _____
c _____ + chip = _____
d _____ + cab = _____
e _____ + phone = _____
f _____ + scope = _____
g _____ + skirt = _____
h _____ + wave = _____

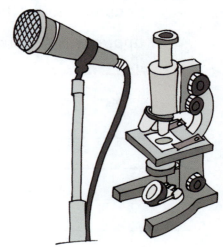

II Choose a suffix *let, ette,* or *ling* to complete these word sums.

a owl + _____ = _____
b sap + _____ = _____
c book + _____ = _____
d cigar + _____ = _____
e kitchen + _____ = _____
f major + _____ = _____
g duck + _____ = _____
h statue + _____ = _____

Speech punctuation

When using speech marks, we have to follow some rules about punctuation and capital letters.

Sometimes we write who is speaking before we write what they say.

> Attia said, 'Let's go and play!'

Put a comma before the speech marks. The full stop, question mark or exclamation mark at the end of the sentence goes inside the speech marks.

Sometimes we write what they say first, then write who is speaking.

> 'Great, let's go,' said Mari.

The first word of a piece of speech always starts with a capital letter.

A comma, question mark or exclamation mark at the end of the speech is used inside the speech marks.

 Look carefully at this piece of writing. Circle the mistakes that have been made with speech marks, punctuation and capital letters.

'Stop! Thief'! yelled the shopkeeper.

Max asked, 'what's the matter?'

'That man stole the money from the till, replied the shopkeeper.'

Max asked ', Which way did he go?'

The shopkeeper said, 'Over the bridge towards the station'.

'I'll follow him, and you phone the police', shouted Max.

'You can't escape', panted Max as he ran after the thief.

'You'll never catch me!,' replied the thief.

 Add the speech marks and punctuation to these sentences.

a Wesley said We're going to Spain on holiday

b Can I have a drink please asked Lola

c Ouch yelled Kira

d Luke asked What time is it

e My big brother shouted Get out

Balanced arguments

A balanced argument needs to include both points of view.

Connectives like **if, also, then, although, however** and **on the other hand**, allow us to compare different points of view.

I think swimming is the best sport. Kelly, **on the other hand**, loves tennis.

I Underline the connectives in this argument.

> If you spend all your pocket money on sweets, then you will not have any left to buy other things. Also, sweets are bad for your teeth.
>
> On the other hand, if you save some of your pocket money you will be able to buy something you really want. Although it can take a while to save enough, it will be worth it in the end.

II Here is an argument about whether children should be allowed to choose when they go to bed. Pick connectives from the box to complete the argument.

| if | then | on the other hand | however | although | also |

_____ children know how tired they feel, they are too young to understand how much sleep they really need. _____ children are allowed to decide when they go to bed, _____ they may be too tired to concentrate at school. _____, tired children can be very bad-tempered, which could cause arguments at home.

_____, being able to choose their own bedtimes may actually save arguments in the family. Children can always catch up with sleep at the weekends. _____, this would use up a lot of their free time.

Alliteration

Alliteration is when several words next to each other, or very close together, begin with the **same sound**.

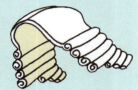
one white wig

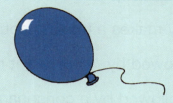
bright blue balloon

Using alliteration draws attention to that part of your writing and helps to add rhythm, especially in poetry.

I Underline the alliteration in each sentence.

a Daisy danced daintily across the stage.

b Crystal the cat crept cautiously to the door.

c Katie bought a pink patterned purse.

d Philip found frogs in the pond.

e Noble knights never run from battle.

f Gemma tells tall tales.

g Rachel's rabbits wriggled in her arms.

h Nasty gnomes never play fair.

II Finish each phrase by adding two more words that start with the same sound.

a beautiful babies _____ _____

b tall trees _____ _____

c honest ogres _____ _____

d sleepy Simon _____ _____

e careful Cara _____ _____

f fat fairies _____ _____

g poor Peter _____ _____

h reckless rhinos _____ _____

More letter strings

Letter strings can make different sounds in different words. This can make spelling difficult. If we look at where the letter string appears in a word, we can find clues to help us.

ss usually makes a **hissing** sound.   di**ss**cu**ss**

If it is followed by *ion* or *ian*, it makes a *sh* sound.   discu**ss**ion

If *wa* is followed by a consonant then *e* or *i*,
it usually makes a *way* sound.   **wa**ve

wai also makes a *way* sound in words.   a**wai**t

But if *wa* is followed by *r* then a consonant, it makes a *war* sound.   **wa**rd

I Underline the words where *ss* makes a *sh* sound.

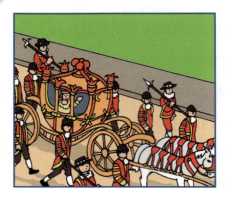

a procession   f session

b lesson   g mission

c hiss   h helpless

d passion   i discussion

e possess   j success

II Sort these words into two groups – one with a *war* sound and one with the *way* sound. Then add two more words to each group.

wake   wage   warn   waif   swarm   towards

war sound   **way** sound

a _____   b _____

_____   _____

_____   _____

_____   _____

_____   _____

Its and it's

Apostrophes are used to shorten and join words together.

> It is my parrot → It's my parrot

They also show when something belongs to someone.

> Sian's parrot.

These are called possessive apostrophes. The only exception is **it**, which never has a possessive apostrophe.

> The parrot flapped its wings.

I Add the apostrophe to **its** in these sentences if it is necessary.

a The cat licked its paws.
b Its my favourite book.
c Its starting to rain.
d The hamster escaped from its cage.
e In the autumn the tree loses its leaves.
f Its easier to roller-skate than ice-skate.
g The dog wagged its tail.

II Rewrite these sentences, replacing the words in bold with **its** or **it's**.

a I like popcorn, because **it is** sweet and crunchy.

_____

b **It is** important to take care when you cross the road.

_____

c The bird flapped **the bird's** wings.

_____

d **It is** hot today.

_____

e When **the clock's** battery ran down, the clock stopped working.

_____

f The flower opened **the flower's** petals.

_____

ANSWERS

Page 2
I Long vowel sounds: a, e, g, h, j
   Short vowel sounds: b, c, d, f, i

II a There are apple and cherry trees in my garden.
   b I grabbed the kitten.
   c My house is more modern than your cottage.
   d John scribbled on the paper.
   e Mum read what was written on the label.
   f The rabbit was running all over the garden.

Page 3
I a new   f heard
   b whole   g see
   c great   h bee
   d their   i four or fore
   e too or to   j right or rite

II Many answers are possible.

Page 4
I a jumping   e shopping
   b looked   f saved, saving
   c touches   g cries, crying
   d grabbed

II a stopped   d washes
   b cooking   e dropped
   c carried   f explores

Page 5
I a partnership f membership
   b kindness   g silliness
   c fitness   h friendship
   d enjoyment   i carelessness
   e willingness j amusement

II a measurement f wickedness
   b tidiness   g fellowship
   c nastiness   h apprenticeship
   d employment   i replacement
   e statement   j championship

Page 6
I a house: a building people live in
   b sheep: a farmyard animal producing wool
   c bed: a piece of furniture used for sleeping on
   d breakfast: the first meal of the day
   e field: a piece of land used for farming
   f apple: a fruit grown on trees
   g winter: the coldest season
   h cow: a farmyard animal producing milk

II Many answers are possible.

Page 7
I a submarine f summer
   b success   g sunny
   c sudden   h super
   d sugar   i suspect
   e suitable

Page 8
I a hail   e harp
   b hair   f haste
   c hard   g hat
   d hare   h have

Page 8 (continued)
I a tight, height, bite, kite, bright
   b moat, boat, stoat, goat, float
   c chair, pair, stair, rare, bear

II Many answers are possible.

Page 9
I a deepen   f elasticate
   b shorten   g purify
   c standardise h formalise
   d apologise   i waken
   e notify   j medicate

II a intensify   f glorify
   b realise   g hasten
   c strengthen   h classify
   d simplify   i serialise
   e harden   j weaken

Page 10
I a hurt   c ran   e sent
   b put   d brought   f fell

II a Yesterday, I ate my birthday cake.
   b Last week, Jamilla bought a comic.
   c Earlier today, Ali drew a picture.
   d Last night, I was tired.
   e When I was four, I could swim.
   f Yesterday, I told you a secret.

Page 11
I a carefully   f happily
   b beautifully g sleepily
   c silently   h angrily
   d lazily   i impatiently
   e badly

II Many answers are possible.

Page 12
I a hobbles shuffles ambles
   b argues   dictates declares
   c devours munches   chews

II The verbs should appear in the following order in the story: ordered, yelled, shot, clambered, crept, gazed, grabbed, fled, hacked, crashed

Page 13
I a After tea, we played football.
   b Find your trainers, Paul.
   c Suddenly, the lights went out.
   d Judy and James, from next door, came shopping with us.
   e My hat, which is black, matches my scarf.
   f Last Tuesday, after school, I went skating.

II a Tomorrow, we are playing football.
   b The ink, which was blue, stained the carpet.
   c Eventually, Jane won the game.
   d It's time to go, Ali.
   e While we were on holiday, we stayed in a hotel.
   f At school, in my classroom, is a display about trains.

Page 14
I The pictures should appear in this order: 2, 5, 3, 6, 1, 4

II a The Smith family moved into their new house on Friday.
   b They spent the weekend unpacking.
   c When they had finished unpacking, Grace realised that a box of her toys was missing.
   d On Monday, Dad phoned the removal company to see if they had the box.
   e The removal company looked in the van and found the box.
   f Many answers are possible.

Page 15
I a sniffs   f scuffs
   b halves   g calves
   c puffs   h thieves
   d cliffs   i yourselves
   e scarves j knives

II a loaves   f wives
   b selves   g bluffs
   c sheriffs h shelves
   d cuffs   i elves
   e wolves   j scoffs

Page 16
I a starving   e terrifying
   b exhausted   f parched
   c lovely   g drenched
   d horrible   h hilarious

II Many answers are possible.

Page 17
I Older words are:
   a, c, d, f, h
   Newer words are:
   b, e, g, i, j

II a We drove in the car.
   b Where did you come from?
   c Look at the amazing sight.
   d Will you stay for a while?
   e Shall we listen to the radio?
   f It was cold, so I wore a scarf.

Page 18
I a shocking   f acidic
   b washable   g roadworthy
   c trustworthy h amusing
   d beautiful   i breakable
   e reliable   j painful